AUGUSTINE FOR EVERYONE

By the same author:

An Augustine Treasury, Boston, 1981.

A Philosopher's Search for the Infinite,
New York, 1983.

An Aquinas Treasury, Arlington, 1988.

Newman for Everyone, New York, 1996.

New Approaches to God, North Andover,
1996.

Augustine for Everyone

101 Questions answered
imaginatively by Augustine

Translated by

JULES M. BRADY, SJ

Professor of Philosophy
Rockhurst University

ST PAULS

Library of Congress Cataloging-in-Publication Data

Augustine, Saint, Bishop of Hippo.
    Augustine for everyone : 101 questions answered imaginatively by
Augustine / translated by Jules M. Brady.
        p. cm.
    Includes bibliographical references.
    ISBN 0-8189-0925-0 (alk. paper)
    1. Theology—Early works to 1800. 2. Catholic Church—Doctrines—
Miscellanea.   I. Brady, Jules M.   II. Title.

    BR65.A52 E6 2002
    230'.14 — dc21   2002018623

Imprimi Potest:
Frank Reale, SJ
Censor Librorum

Produced and designed in the United States of America by the
Fathers and Brothers of the Society of St. Paul,
2187 Victory Boulevard, Staten Island, New York 10314-6603,
as part of their communications apostolate.

ISBN: 0-8189-0925-0

Printing Information:

Current Printing - first digit   1   2   3   4   5   6   7   8   9   10

Year of Current Printing - first year shown

2002   2003   2004   2005   2006   2007   2008   2009   2010

Dedicated to my former students

Beth Bernskoetter
Melissa Fortmann
Jacki Prosperi Gunn
Ami Leiendecker Kohlberg
Malissa Ross
Teresa Vondrak

Acknowledgments

The readings in this volume are translated from the following writings by St. Augustine.

On Catechizing the Uninstructed
Christian Combat
City of God
Confessions
Epistle of John to the Parthians
Against Faustus the Manichee
Letters
On the Psalms
On St. John's Gospel
Sermons
On the Soul and Its Origin
On the Spirit and the Letter
On the Trinity

Contents

I. God

II. Evil

III. Self

IV. Teaching

V. Death

VI. Heaven

VII. Happiness

VIII. Sin

IX. Grace

X. Faith

XI. Love of Neighbor

XII. Use of Creatures

XIII. Peace

XIV. Wisdom

XV. Prayer

XVI. Christ

XVII. Mass

Preface

Augustine for Everyone contains topics with concrete images taken from St. Augustine's writings, originally composed in Latin, and translated into readable English. Augustine provides the theme and the example. I have rendered the passages into English easy to understand.

St. Augustine's books are beautiful for two reasons. First, during his youth he was trained to be a rhetoric teacher. Secondly, from the time he was consecrated Bishop of Hippo in 396 until his death in 430 he wrote sermons on the Psalms and the Gospel of St. John in addition to many other books. It is no wonder that a pastor who combined the skills of a rhetorician and scripture scholar wrote such beautiful religious books that continue to be read down to the present day.

This little book, exemplifying how Augustine expressed Christ's call to everyone, has three purposes. First, it may provide subjects for daily meditation. Second, it may assist a priest preparing a homily. Third, it may encourage the reader to read the great books of St. Augustine: the *Confessions* and the *City of God*.

St. Augustine of Hippo

In 354 A.D. Augustine was born in Tagaste, a North African city in the Roman province of Numidia. Today named Souk Ahras in modern Algeria, it is about thirty miles south of the Mediterranean Sea.

Augustine's complexion was dark, like the Arabs of North Africa of today. Patricius, his father, a pagan, was a descendent of Roman colonists. A tax collector, he owned a forty-acre estate and raised horses. Patricius became a Christian just before he died in 372.

St. Monica, St. Augustine's mother, was a native of North Africa and a devout Catholic. She did not have much initial influence on her son because, according to the custom, the father was responsible for the education of his sons.

In 366 Augustine began attending a school in Madera. There he learned to write Latin fluently. In 370 he moved to Carthage and began living with a girl without marriage. They had a son, Adeodatus, born in 372. He spent four years there teaching rhetoric, having majored in forensics, literature and philosophy. While in Carthage, he received several prizes for his erudition and his eloquence. He also joined a pseudo-Christian sect, the Manicheans.

In 383, Augustine went to Rome where he taught philosophy for a year or so. When some Roman Manichean friends managed to obtain a position for him as public speaker in Milan, the headquarters of the Emperor, he took his family and moved north. In Milan Augustine by chance heard St. Ambrose, the Bishop of the city, preach. His rhetoric impressed him very much. By this time Augustine had read the whole New Testament but did not understand it.

In the meantime, St. Monica had followed her son to Milan and urged him to send his mistress back to Africa. Augustine yielded to his mother's request and dismissed the girl. Although by this time he had left the Manicheans, he still had intellectual difficulties with the Christian faith. In a famous conversion experience, he obeyed the suggestion of a voice he heard while walking in a garden, "Take and read." Augustine read the following passage from St. Paul's letter to the Romans, 13:13-14: "Let us conduct ourselves decently as we would during the day, not in carousing and drunkenness, not in promiscuity and indecent behavior, not in strife and envy. Instead clothe yourselves with the Lord Jesus Christ and give no thought to doing what the flesh desires." As a result of this reading Augustine decided to become a Christian. In 387 he was baptized at the age of 33.

Shortly thereafter he decided to move back to Africa, taking with him his brother, his son and his mother. On the way, at Ostia where they awaited a ship for the return trip, Augustine had a spiritual conversation with Monica, in which she expressed her readiness to die, requesting only that Augustine pray daily for her soul. Within days she died and was buried in Italy.

Back in his native Africa, Augustine was ordained a priest in 391, and in 396 he was consecrated Bishop of Hippo Regius, a city on the Mediterranean Sea. In 399 he wrote the *Confessions*, and between 413 and 426 he composed the *City of God.* During his years as Bishop he wrote a vast number of works on various subjects, including his commentary on St. John's Gospel and another commentary on the Psalms. He died in 430 at the age of 76 as the Vandals were attacking Hippo.

Christopher Dawson in *St. Augustine and His Age* comments that Augustine "was, to a far greater degree than any emperor or barbarian war-lord, a maker of history and a builder of the bridge which was to lead the old world to the new."

AUGUSTINE FOR EVERYONE

· I ·

God

1. How can we know that God is love?

We cannot see God. But from the effects of love in a human person we can come to some kind of knowledge of love. It is love that impels feet to go to church, that moves hands to feed the poor, that focuses eyes on the needs of others, that turns ears to listen to a sermon. Anyone whose love of God prompts the above effects knows what love is. Yet God is love without feet, without hands, without eyes and without ears. God's love is invisible.

Epistle of John to the Parthians 7, 10

2. How can the beauty of the universe inspire us to praise God's Beauty?

The pleasure we experience in seeing a beautiful cathedral reminds us to admire the church's architect. How much more should viewing the universe's infinite variety stir us to praise the Beauty of its Creator. Consider, for a moment, the whole of creation. The splendor of the starry skies, the various colors in a flower garden, the stately majesty of a cluster of trees, the melodious songs of birds, the variations of creatures in the animal kingdom, the sense and intellectual faculties of a human person, are like so many voices that praise the Beauty of their Author. Words fail us in our effort to describe adequately what the beauty of the universe tells us of the Divine Artist's Beauty. Does triumphant music come closer to express God's Beauty?

On Psalm 26

3. From the works of creation how do I know the Creator?

When I see someone, I see the individual's body but not the soul. However, since the same person speaks, walks, works, it is by these visible operations of the body that I know this individual has an invisible soul. So, too, from the visible works of creation I know there is an invisible Creator.

On Psalm 74

4. How can the eyes of the body arouse the eye of reason to know the Author of creation?

God has given us eyes in the body and reason in the heart. Use the eyes of the body to see what is visible: heaven and earth, the ornaments of the sky, the fruits of the earth, the flight of birds, the swimming of fish, the seasons of the year. Then, with the eye of reason seek to know what is invisible: the Author of the works of creation.

Sermon 76

5. *How may we think of God?*

The way we think about our own act of reasoning, the best part of our being, is similar to the manner in which we may describe God, a far better being than our own act of reasoning. Do we notice in our own act of reasoning a definite shape, a beautiful color, a great space, an extended size, or movement through place? What we don't find in our own act of reasoning we ought not to look for in God. Therefore, let us think of God as follows: as great without external shape, as beautiful without color, as being everywhere without space, as a Creator who contains all things but without a position, and who makes and rules all changeable things without change in Himself. Whoever thinks of God in this way won't know everything about God but will avoid making errors about Him.

On the Trinity 5, 1.2

6. *How is God present in the world?*

The carpenter is external to the chest that he builds. Even while he makes it, the carpenter is in one place and the chest is in another place. On the other hand, God is internal to the world He continually creates. God is not in one place and the world in another place. He is everywhere present to the world He fashions. By His presence God not only makes the world but also governs what He is creating. Therefore, God is continually in the world as the Maker of the world.

On the Gospel of John 2, 10

7. *How is God present to the believer and to the unbeliever?*

The sun shines on both the blind and those that see. But there is a difference. The blind person does not see; but the person with eyesight sees. In like manner, God illumines with the ray of faith both the unbeliever and the believer. Again there is a difference. The closed eyes of the unbeliever's mind do not understand; but the sound eyes of the believer's mind do understand.

On the Gospel of John 35, 4

8. *How is the Word of God present to us?*

When we speak to an audience of several people, those present hear all that we say. They do not divide the sounds among themselves into particles as if they were after dinner treats. Rather, each person hears wholly the whole sound of a voice. In like manner, as the sound of a voice is heard entirely by each person, the Word is everywhere totally present.

Letter 137

9. *Why is God present differently in each person?*

A sound is not received by a deaf person, is not received entirely by a partially deaf person, is received completely by those who hear, although the sound itself does not vary but is equally present to all. How much more perfect is God who cannot be divided like sound into temporal intervals but who can be wholly present to all persons, although they possess Him in proportion to their own capacities.

Letter 187, 19

10. *Did the creature exist in the Word before it exists in reality?*

The design of a building existed in the architect's mind before the building exists in reality. Likewise, every creature exists in the Word before it exists in reality.

On Psalm 45, 5

11. *Why is God more beautiful than the sun?*

There are two reasons for this. First, when the sun rises, it lights up the earth; it illumines colors; it shines through windows; but it cannot penetrate walls. However, God is present in all places, even in a wall. Secondly, when the sun rises in the East, it is absent from the West. When the sun sets in the West, it is away from the East. At night the sun is not seen. However, when God is in the East, He is also in the West. When He is in the West, He is likewise in the East. He is also present at night. He is whole everywhere. If the sun is beautiful, how much more beautiful is God, the sun's Maker.

Sermon 70, 2

12. *What is the Word of God?*

Compare a spoken word with the Word of God, the Second Person of the Trinity. What happens when I speak a word about the Word? The word I speak to you reaches all of you. You did not divide what I said to you. If I gave you loaves of bread, all the loaves could not be eaten by each of you. You would divide the loaves among yourselves. How different is the word I speak to you. It comes whole to each of you; all of you receive the whole word. You do not divide the word. And yet, what I spoke has not been separated from me. But it has reached you. In other words, I have lost nothing; and you have received the whole word. What a marvel is the spoken word! Yet, how much more marvelous is the Word of God Who is Whole everywhere.

Sermon 70

13. *Is the Creator superior to the creature?*

The carpenter is greater than the wooden bench he crafted; and yet, even though the artisan assembled the wood into the shape of a bench out of existing wooden planks, the wood worker did not create the wood. On the other hand, the Creator made a creature out of no pre-existing material because He created the creature's total being. Therefore, the Creator is on a higher level than the creature, the carpenter.

On the Gospel of John 42, 10

14. *How can we know the Holy Spirit?*

I know the Holy Spirit the way I know my own conscience. Both are in me and both are invisible. But there is a difference. My conscience is only within me. However, the Holy Spirit dwells in me and is also apart from me.

On the Gospel of John 74, 5

15. *How do the words spoken by John in the desert resemble the Word?*

John's spoken words have two aspects. First, these words are expressed orally by John's voice. This voice ceases at the end of John's discourse. Secondly, these words have a meaning which is continuous between John's mind and the listener's mind after the voice ceases.

Certainly, the voice of those spoken words do not resemble the Word. For the voice ceases at the end of John's sermon. And the Word is eternal.

Now, only the meaning of those spoken words are like the Word. The reason is that this meaning is continuous in the mind of John and in the mind of the audience. Of course, the Word is eternal.

Therefore, not the sound of John's voice but its meaning resembles the eternal Word of God.

Sermon 293, 3

16. *How can we love God?*

Earthly love and divine love cannot dwell in the same breast. An apostle wants to cleanse our hearts of earthly love so that we can love God.

Such an apostle sees a human heart as a field covered with weeds. These weeds are the love of the world. This apostle would root up all the weeds so that the apostle may plant charity, the love of God.

Then our hearts will be empty of earthly love; and divine love may live in our hearts.

Epistle of John to the Parthians 2, 8

17. *Why does the love of God surpass all other loves?*

Some endure toil, dangers, troubles, for the love of money. But at the same time, they may lose sleep for fear of thieves. Others ask an inferior to secure the love of a powerful friend. God says to us: "Love Me and I am with you." There love is without toil, without dangers, without troubles, without fear of thieves, and without the assistance of a go-between. This love surpasses all other loves.

Epistle of John to the Parthians 10, 4

· II ·

Evil

18. *How can the same affliction prompt the wicked to curse God and inspire the good to praise Him?*

The same fire causes straw to smoke and gold to gleam. The same press threshes the grain and crushes the stalk. So, the same trouble worsens the wicked and improves the good. Consequently, the difference between the wicked and the good is not what they suffer but the way they suffer. Therefore, the same evil incites the wicked to deny God and stirs the good to pray to Him.

City of God 1, 8

19. *What is the sleep of the soul?*

God has given us sleep of the body in order to insure the health of the body. Without this sleep, the body occupied with many active pursuits may faint. Therefore sleep of the body is good.

We must be careful that our soul does not sleep but rather watches for God. For the sleep

of the soul is to forget God. Therefore, the sleep
of the soul is evil.

On Psalm 53, 2

20. *Should we blame Scripture because God's*
    forgiveness of David's sin may encourage
    others to sin?

We don't fault surgery if an insane person uses
surgical instruments to harm another person.
And so we don't fault Scripture if a sinner fails
to read Scripture's remedy for pardoning sin.
David's repentance is a great example not to in-
jure the healthy but to help the sick.

Against Faustus the Manichee 22, 97

21. *Why does God send hardships to holy persons?*

Trees in the winter are without leaves and fruit.
When the spring comes the tree becomes alive
with new leaves and fresh fruit.

Holy people may experience sufferings in
this life. But the Just God will make sure that
they will have many consolations.

On Psalm 36, *Sermon* 3, 9

22. *Why does God allow tribulations to happen to us?*

Because we cannot endure perpetually the hardships of life, we seek rest in some earthly thing. It may be our house, our family, our children, a little farm, an orchard, or a book we have published. God allows us to suffer tribulations even in these innocent delights in order that we may love only life eternal. Otherwise, as travelers going to their country, we might choose the inn — this world — instead of our true home: eternal life.

On Psalm 41, 4

23. *Does God scourge His own servants?*

God scourged His own Son whom He received into Paradise. Therefore, God allows His servants to be tempted so that they may not suffer eternal punishment but may attain the happiness of Heaven.

On Psalm 80, 4

24. *Why does God send trials to His saints?*

While the unskillful pronounce a work of art — a painting, a sculpture, a building — perfect, the artist continues to polish them. The unskillful wonder why these art pieces receive additional polish. The judgment of the inexperienced is one thing, the rule of art is another. Likewise, someone noticing the sufferings of a saint questions why God continues to afflict such a holy person. God so acts not to punish the saint for sins but to purify the saint's affections, and thus to remove imperfections. How did God try holy people like Samuel and Aaron? God compelled them to live among people who did not live holy lives.

On Psalm 99, 10

25. How can we explain the physical evils in the world?

An unskilled person entering a carpenter's shop will understand that each tool hanging on the wall has a definite purpose. Likewise, a person of faith will acknowledge that hail, snow, ice, storms, floods occur for a reason: God commands them to happen because God is so powerful that He will bring good from evil.

On Psalm 148, 9

26. How can I cross the ocean of this world and arrive safely at the harbor of eternal life?

If I try by myself to swim across the ocean of this world, the waves will certainly engulf me. In order to survive I must climb aboard a ship made of wood; this wood is the Cross of Christ.

Of course, even on board ship there will be dangerous tempests and perils from the sea of this world. But God will help me remain on board the ship and arrive safely at the harbor of eternal life.

Sermon 25, 2

27. *How does God bring good out of evil?*

Suppose a thief breaks into a home. Subsequently, a justice official apprehends the culprit, and brings the guilty person before a court of law. The judge sentences the criminal to cut square stones from a quarry. Then the town architect uses these cut stone blocks to ornament a public building. Breaking into a house is evil; ornamenting a civic hall is good. God has drawn good out of evil.

Sermon 75, 5

28. *How is a Christian similar to a squared stone?*

If you turn over a squared stone, the stone remains erect. When trials, as it were, turn a Christian over, the Christian does not fall down but stands erect.

On Psalm 87, 3

· III ·

Self

29. Why is there discord between my body and my mind?

One day I noticed an apple on my neighbor's tree. My mind ordered my hand to pick the apple; at the same time my mind commanded itself not to take the apple. And yet, my hand grabbed the apple; and my mind disobeyed itself. Why does this discord occur between my body and my mind? Is this conflict not one of the results of Adam's sin?

Confessions 8, 2

30. Am I present more to myself than to another?

I am present to myself not by looking at my face unless I look into a mirror. But I am present to myself by looking into my conscience which I can know even if I close my eyes.

Therefore, I am present more to myself than to another physically present to me because I know my internal thoughts which another person cannot see.

Letter 267

31. Why should the beauty of a just person please us?

The beauty of a church with its marble pillars and gold ceilings pleases the eyes of the body. Yet, an elderly person, bent over, with a wrinkled brow, gray hair, and missing teeth, does not please the bodily eyes.

However, if this same person is just, covets no person's goods, distributes goods to the needy, gives sound advice, and believes the entire faith, such a person has an inner beauty that pleases the inner eye. That is why the martyrs, torn apart by wild beasts and covered with wounds, were a bloody spectacle. But these same martyrs had an inner beauty of justice that not only pleased the inner eye but also won the affections of anyone witnessing the ordeal.

On Psalm 65, 8

32. Why is it profitable to lead a good life?

Words written by a pen on a wax tablet are easily blotted out. But a good life lived according to God's commands are like words written by a pen on our hearts, our character. They will never be erased.

On Psalm 94, 25

33. Why is the soul not a body?

The soul is not a body. For the soul is not air; and air is a body. An experiment proves that air is a body. If you lower an empty vessel with mouth downward straight into the water, no water enters because the air keeps the water out. However, if you lower a vessel on a slant, it fills with water since at the same opening the air escapes as the water comes in. Now the soul is not air. Therefore it is not a body.

Soul and Its Origin 4, 18

34. Why is a forbidden evil act more alluring?

A rushing stream meeting an obstacle becomes more violent; when it has overcome the impediment the water increases its force as it flows towards its destination. In a similar way, when the Holy Spirit no longer stirs us to do a good act, the very forbidding of an evil act increases our eagerness to perform the evil act.

On the Spirit and the Letter, 6

35. Why does God, at times, frighten me and, at other times, fascinate me?

When I observe how different I am from God, I tremble. But when I notice how similar I am to God, I am set on fire. Therefore, God at times frightens me and, at other times, fascinates me.

Confessions 11,11

· IV ·

Teaching

36. Why should teachers joyfully teach others the paths to peace?

Anyone walking through the streets of a familiar city always is delighted to stop and to answer questions of strangers about directions. How much more cheerfully ought a teacher of Christian doctrine, over and over again, escort along the paths to peace persons dissatisfied with the world.

On Catechizing the Uninstructed 12, 17

37. What is the secret of successful teaching?

When we show out of town friends a city's beautiful sights that we have often noticed without any pleasure, we experience delight by the delight our friends have for these scenes. So it is that a teacher, teaching a familiar topic to students who are thrilled by learning something new, experiences renewed pleasure in teaching the subject. The greater the bond of friendship between teacher and student, the greater will be the love the teacher has for teaching and the greater will be the love the students have for learning.

On Catechizing the Uninstructed 12, 17

38. *Why does an allegorical presentation of doctrine please the listener more than doctrine explained in plain words?*

A torch that is shaken bursts into flames. Similarly, truths adorned with figures enkindle love.

Letter 55

· V ·

Death

39. *Why should we not fear death?*

Sunset is not the end of daylight but soon after
the dawn of a new day. So, death for a person
united with Christ is not the end of a good life
but the onset of a better life. Any misfortune that
comes to the dying is not due to their death but
due to their life.

Letter 151 to Caecilian

40. *How can I console a person grieving over the*
death of a best friend?

Whoever loves gold, does not lose the gold by
putting it in a safe. Even though such a person
does not see the gold, this individual feels more
secure about it.

When a person loves a best friend, the person does not lose the friend who is safe in
heaven. Even though the person does not see
the best friend, the person feels more certain
about the friend's salvation. They still love each
other. And this love is hidden in Christ.

After all, Christ dies for me; I no longer see

Him. But I know that we mutually love each other.

Thoughts such as these are divine consolations that may change sadness into joy.

Letter 263

Heaven

41. How can we repay the Divine Physician for healing our inner sight, enabling us to behold the Eternal Light which is Himself?

Suppose a physician heals a blind person so that such a person, for the first time, sees the light of day. What gift could the patient possibly give the doctor that would equal the gift of sight? Even gold would not be an adequate repayment for such a gift.

What gift can we give the Divine Physician for curing our inner sight so that we can behold the Eternal Light of Heaven?

On Psalm 67, 1

42. How can we describe our entrance into Heaven?

During the winter we may observe two trees. Both trees appear dead because both trees are without leaves and fruit.

How can we tell if the trees are alive or dead? We must wait for the summer. Then the living tree will have beautiful leaves and delicious fruit. But the dead trees will lack both leaves and fruit.

The same is true of two human persons. Both are born, grow, consume food and drink. Both wear clothes and live their lives until they die. They are living during the winter of their lives.

Summer comes when both persons die; and the Lord will come. Then the person who has turned away from God in this life will not be clothed in Eternal Light. But the person who has spent the winter of life turned toward God will be illumined with the Sun of Righteousness for all eternity.

On Psalm 148, 10

43. *How may we describe the eternal inheritance of the just?*

On this earth only when parents die do children possess their parents' inheritance.

But in Heaven, what an inheritance do the members of Christ possess? They possess the inheritance of their Heavenly Father who does not die. Even more, their Father will Himself be their inheritance.

Sermon 96, 1

44. *Can prayerful persons in this life ever catch a brief experience of the joys of Heaven?*

In Heaven, due to joy in the presence of God's face, there is a never ending festival of music and song. For a brief time, when the clouds disperse, prayerful persons hear the melodious sounds of the heavenly choirs. Yet, at length, the world drowns out the sounds; the clouds close over; and prayerful persons lapse back to their ordinary states.

On Psalm 42, 8

45. *How can I help others love God?*

If I admire a tenor in an opera, I shall want to be friends with all my associates who like the same tenor. My enthusiasm may reach such a pitch that I shall try to encourage others to listen to the tenor sing.

Correspondingly, if I love God, I should want to be with friends in love with God. Should I not want others to love God who will give to those that love Him peace in this life and everlasting happiness, Himself, in the next life?

Christian Doctrine 1, 29

46. *How did Christ teach us not to seek earthly
    happiness but to strive for eternal happiness?*

In His life on earth Christ received insults, con-
tempt, scourging, a crown of thorns, crucifixion,
and death. In this way He taught His followers
that the purpose of life is to serve God not for
temporal happiness but for eternal life.

Letter 140, 5 *to Honoratus*

· VII ·

Happiness

47. *Why may a good person in tribulation find happiness?*

A carpenter seeing the rotten surface of a tree may find that the inner marrow of the tree is sound. He won't be anxious about the injured surface of the tree; but he knows the sound wood may be used in the construction of a building. So, a person suffering momentary losses or ill health yet with a good conscience will not be upset by outer trials but will flee to his conscience and find God.

On Psalm 46, 3

48. *Does perfect happiness consist in possessing temporal goods?*

A fish delighted by devouring the bait and not noticing the hook, for awhile takes pleasure in the bait; but when the fisherman begins to pull in the line, the hook draws the fish to its destruction away from its joy in consuming the bait. A person imagining that perfect happiness comes from temporal goods has a similar fate. For awhile the person wanders about delighting in temporal goods; but at length the person will feel the anguish caused by greediness. On the other hand, a good person possesses the Object of true happiness, and no one can separate this person from the Good loved.

Christian Combat 7, 8

· VIII ·

Sin

49. Why should I avoid the smallest sins?

Bits of grain accumulated make up a mass of grain; the smallest drops develop into a river. Therefore I should avoid the smallest daily sins.

On Psalm 94, 5

50. How does a bad conscience affect a person?

Any person dwelling in a house suddenly filled with smoke quickly runs outdoors in order to escape the odor. In like manner, a person oppressed within by a bad conscience leaves the inner self in an effort to find rest without in exterior trifles and luxuries. Because all is not well within, such a person wishes to be well without.

On Psalm 101, 3

51. Do sins mar the beauty of God's universe?

Dark colors in their proper places do not dim the clarity, proportion and integrity of a beautiful painting. And so sins, even if they are unsightly marks, do not diminish the beauty of God's universe planned according to His just laws.

City of God 11, 23

Grace

52. How can we overcome the sadness resulting from our sin?

When fire breaks out in a building we are grateful to any person showing us water with which to put out the blaze.

If the straw of our passions becomes inflamed by sin, we would be thankful if someone would suggest a work of great mercy that would quench the flame of sin.

On Catechizing the Uninstructed 14, 22

53. Why did Adam justly incur a penalty for deserting God?

There is a positive and a negative aspect in the life of a human person. To keep oneself alive is a positive act not subject to choice but possible only by taking nourishment. On the other hand, to choose not to live is a negative act which can be freely willed, as occurs in suicide.

In a parallel fashion, for Adam to live according to God's will was not subject to choice and depended on God's grace. Yet, for Adam to

disobey God was our first parent's choice. Therefore Adam justly deserved a penalty for not
obeying God.

City of God 14, 27

54. *How can I overcome the evil habit of telling lies?*

As long as snow remains snow, it cannot become
warm. When the sun melts the snow, the snow
becomes warm.

Suppose a person voluntarily begins to
experience the pleasure of telling lies, a habit is
lodged in the mind causing the tongue with
difficulty to speak the truth. If the person de-
cides to speak truthfully, the mind of the flesh
wars against the soul, and the person is habitu-
ated to telling lies. However, if the soul has been
illuminated by God, the soul is no longer the
mind of the flesh but is subject to God's law and
forms the good habit of speaking the truth.

Disputation Against Fortunatus 22

55. *How can our mind discover how God wants us to live?*

In order to see light there are two requirements.
First, we must have sound eyes that are open.
Secondly, we need the help of sunshine in order
to see the colors of the world.

Similarly, our mind is called the eye of the soul. Even blind Tobit had the eye of the soul. Second, the light of truth shines on the eye of the soul and points out God's way of living. Thus the light of Truth illuminated blind Tobit so that by holding his son's hand, he indicated God's way of living to his son.

Therefore, to find out how God wants us to live there are two requisites. First, we require our mind, the eye of the soul. Second, the light of Truth must illumine that eye and point out God's will to us.

On the Gospel of John 35, 3

56. *How can God take the initiative in loving the unjust since Scripture says God hates iniquity?*

A good doctor both loves and hates a sick person. The physician loves the sick person in order to remove illness from such a person and also hates the sick person because of the person's illness.

On Patience 22, 19

57. *How does God forgive our sins?*

The cold weather freezes water into ice preventing the water from flowing. When the warm south wind blows, the ice melts forming winter torrents gushing with great force. Likewise, when our sins have frozen us into a block of ice, the south wind of the Holy Spirit warms the ice and our sins melt away. The Holy Spirit has forgiven our sins.

On Psalm 126

58. *How can we tame our tongue?*

The horse, the camel, the elephant do not tame themselves; a human person tames them. So also we do not tame our own tongue; we must ask God to help us tame our tongue.

Sermon 5, 2

59. *How does God help us do a good deed?*

The light of grace coming from God has two effects. First, if we turn toward God, the light of grace enables us to do a lawful deed. Second, if we turn away from God, the light of grace helps us turn toward God.

Corporeal light has only one effect. If our eyes are opened, corporeal light is necessary for us to see colored items. But if our eyes are closed, bodily light does not help us open our eyes.

On the Merits and Remission of Sins and Infant Baptism 2, 5

· X ·

Faith

60. How may Christ dwell in your heart by faith?

When the Apostles were sailing in a ship, the winds and waves arose to such an extent that the vessel was in danger of capsizing. Meanwhile, Christ, oblivious of the storm, was sleeping in the ship. The Apostles came to Christ and awakened Him. He arose, commanded the storm to subside and a great calm followed.

It is likewise with you. Your heart is your ship. The winds enter and toss the vessel of your heart. What are the winds? They are the insults you may have received from another person. You are ready to render cursing for the insult because Christ is sleeping in your heart. The sleep of Christ is the forgetfulness of faith. If you awaken Christ, that is, remember your faith, you will recall that Christ prayed for those insulting Him. Your faith calms the storm and there is tranquillity. Thus Christ is dwelling in your heart by faith.

On the Gospel of John 49, 19

· XI ·

Love of Neighbor

61. How did my mother, Monica, reconcile enemies?

I have experienced that some people, hearing sour gossip from angry enemies, not only run to these enemies with the statements they heard, but even add recriminations not spoken.

My mother was a peacemaker between persons in discord. When she heard bitter remarks from two persons about each other, she would not reveal to the persons involved anything she had heard. Instead, she tried to extinguish the disagreement by gentle conversation.

Confessions 9, 9

62. How may we love an enemy?

Suppose a carpenter walking through a forest sees a tree trunk, unhewn, cut down, lying on the ground. The artisan loves the piece of timber at first sight not because of the wood's present state, but because properly crafted the trunk will become part of a building. So, when meeting an enemy insulting you, there is a way

of loving the enemy at first meeting, not by noticing the insulting remarks but by remember-
ing that humble prayer may change the mali-
cious person into your friend. You love the enemy not as a hostile person but as a future friend.

Epistle of John to the Parthians 8, 10

63. *How should we love our neighbor?*

A physician loves a sick person because the doctor wants the patient to enjoy good health but
not to continue being ill.

Correspondingly, we should love our
neighbor in order that our neighbor might have
God within but not for a worldly purpose.

On the Gospel of John 65, 2

64. *Whom should we love first?*

A nurse in a children's ward loves the weak because they are more in need of help, before car-
ing for the strong.

Likewise, we should love those most in
need of assistance, before looking after those
capable of helping themselves.

Letter 139 *to Marcellinus*

65. Should we love an evil person?

We love a sick person that such a one may recover and not remain ill.

In a similar way, we love an evil person that the individual may become virtuous and not remain evil.

Letter 153 *to Macedonius*

· XII ·

Use of Creatures

66. *What kinds of persons should I cultivate as friends?*

Suppose you meet a person whose beautiful color and symmetrical shape attract your eyes. Yet, when you learn the person is a thief, you will have nothing to do with such an individual.

On the other hand, you may encounter an elderly person, leaning on a cane, hardly able to walk, covered with wrinkles. Moreover, if you find out the person is just, you will want such a one as your friend.

On the Gospel of John 3, 21

67. *How may a religious live a happy community life?*

To avoid a great wave of the ocean and to have a calm sea on which to drop anchor, ships enter a harbor. Yet since the port has an entrance, a strong wind may come into the haven and dash one ship against another until they are all shattered.

To avoid noisy crowds and the waves of

life and to live a quiet, peaceful life free from
the bustle of crowds, a few persons may enter
the threshold of a monastery. Here there is joy
and jubilant gladness provided by the members
loving each other. The person presiding over
such a community will be careful to admit no
evil person. However someone promising to live
a holy life may enter the religious community
and shatter the peace of the community by
selfish behavior.

Where can a person be certain of living in
a peaceful environment? Nowhere in this life.
Complete peace is attained only after we enter
Heaven and the gates are shut. Then we shall
enjoy great delight and full jubilation.

On Psalm 100, 8

68. *How should a person use the creatures of this world?*

Suppose a skilled jeweler crafted a gold wed-
ding ring and gave it to his bride during their
marriage ceremony. As they continued their
married life together, what would you think of
a wife who gradually loved her bridal ring more
than her husband?

And yet, God made the sky, the sea, the
moon, the stars, and beautiful human beings.
Any person loving creatures made by God more
than the Creator would be similar to the wife

loving the ring made by her husband more than her husband himself.

Epistle of John to the Parthians 2, 11

69. How can we use creatures to love God?

When we are traveling we spend the night at an inn. We use money to buy dinner and to pay the room charge. Our purpose is not to stay at the inn but to depart on the following day and continue our journey. If we ask God's help, He will help us use money and the goods of this life not to remain with them but to use them as a means of pressing onward toward the love of God.

On the Gospel of John 40, 10.

70. How can we love God instead of loving the world?

If my hand is holding a heavy book, it cannot hold another heavy object at the same time. I must first put down the book in order to receive a heavy gift package. My love is the hand of my soul. It cannot love God and the world at the same time. It must first cease loving the world in order to love God.

Sermon 75, 7

71. Why should we imitate the humble and not the proud?

The humble resemble a rock. Even though the rock lies downward, it is nevertheless firm. The proud are like smoke. Even though the smoke is lofty, eventually it vanishes.

On Psalm 93, 3

72. Why did David, the sinner, enjoy more divine favor than a just person?

Farmers, removing great thistles from a field that yields a hundredfold, are more pleased with this field than with another field without thistles yielding only thirtyfold. Likewise, David, an adulterer, a murderer, having great sorrow for his sins, pleased God more than another person who never committed adultery or murder, but lacked great sorrow for sins.

Against Faustus the Manichee 22, 68

73. How may Christ help us forgive an enemy?

If an enemy asks our pardon, we must forgive immediately. But when hatred instead of forgiveness is our response to an enemy pleading pardon, what should we do? We must remember that Christ said, "Father, forgive them, for they know not what they do" (Lk 23:34).

We may reflect that Christ, being God, pardoned an enemy; but how can we, sinful persons, extend pardon? Then we should recall that Stephen pardoned those who were stoning him, saying, "Lord, lay not this sin to their charge" (Ac 7:60).

We should imitate Stephen, lift up our hearts, and love our enemies. If we fail to forgive, Christ will blot us out of the book of God.

Sermon 6, 16

· XIII ·

Peace

74. *How do we describe the peace we shall have in Heaven?*

In this world we have a two-fold peace from Christ, our Peace. First, we have peace within in so far as we live in conformity with God's will. This peace is not complete because we experience the struggle going on between our lower nature and our higher nature. Second, we have peace with others when we mutually love others. Here again, the peace is not complete since we do not know another's thoughts.

In Heaven our peace will be complete. For we shall have no internal discord; and we shall know the secret thoughts of others.

On the Gospel of John 77, 4

· XIV ·

Wisdom

75. How does Wisdom come to a person?

A person walking from the interior of a very dark cave to the exit experiences more and more light as the individual approaches the brightness of the entrance to the cavern. In like manner, Wisdom does not come to a person suddenly but rather gradually, as the individual progresses from the darkness of ignorance towards the light of Truth.

Letter 167

· XV ·

Prayer

76. Why should we recite the Apostles' Creed daily?

When we rise in the morning we dress our body in order to prepare for the day's occupation. Appropriately, daily repetition of the Apostles' Creed dresses the soul so that we may always have an interior mirror reflecting the truths of our faith. This mirror is a source of our joy and a breastplate against adversity. When we see God, we shall not have to say the Creed. Our vision of God will reward us for our present faith.

Sermon 8, 13

77. Does God hear our prayers?

If you are ill, you may ask the doctor for some cold water. If it will improve your health, the physician will give you some water at once. But, if the cold water will harm you, the doctor will refuse your request. The doctor certainly heard your request. In like manner, when you petition God for a favor, if it is good for you, God will grant your request at once. If the favor is not for your benefit, the Divine Physician will not accede to your wishes. You may be sure that God heard your prayer.

Epistle of John to the Parthians 6, 8

78. *Why should a faithful person daily pray for forgiveness?*

A ship may sink either by one giant wave or by water entering a small hole in the bottom of the vessel which, being overlooked by the crew, brings the boat to the bottom of the sea.

Likewise, a faithful person may perish either due to one unforgiven serious sin or because of slight offenses caused by human weakness, and which, if unforgiven, would add up to one great sin.

Therefore a faithful person should daily ask God to forgive slight offenses. Thus the prayer "forgive us our offenses as we forgive those who offend us" will take away small sins.

Letter 265 *to Seleuciana*

79. *What should I ask for from God?*

If the Emperor told you, "Ask what you will," perhaps you would request a tribuneship, a chief office of the state or external wealth.

Almighty God says, "Ask what you will," and you might ask for the whole earth, the sea, the air, the heavens, the sun, the moon and the stars. They are all beautiful; but they are made by God. Ask for God Himself and you will have God, Beauty in Itself. And in Him you will possess everything He has made. God loves you and wishes to give you Himself more than anything else.

On Psalm 34, Sermon 1, 12

80. How can we prevent sins from destroying our friendship with God?

If a ship sailing on the sea develops small holes in the hold, the crew will pump out the water lest the water accumulate and sink the ship.

After baptism, through human frailty, we acquire defilements. The collection of these sins may cause us to lose our friendship with God. To avoid this loss we must pump out daily the evil contracted by our sins. We remove them by using our voices and our hands. We employ our voices when we pray, "Forgive us our trespasses as we forgive those who trespass against us." We work with our hands by giving alms to the poor.

Sermon 6, 11

· XVI ·

Christ

81. Why may Christ correct you?

We may notice a person robbing a store and not being apprehended. We may even complain that no one punishes the robber.

If you want the criminal to correct the hand that robbed the store, you should first correct your tongue.

If you want the culprit to have a heart that loves other persons, you must turn your heart to Christ. If you don't, perhaps Christ will correct you before correcting the robber.

On Psalm 94

82. Why did Mary choose the better part?

From the top of a hill the rain flows down to the valley. Just as more water collects at the bottom of the hill, so Mary, sitting in a low place at the feet of Jesus, listening to His words, receives more than Martha, standing and serving the temporal needs of her Master. Mary, loving Jesus, the one thing needed, is in port. Martha, occupying herself about many things, is still at sea.

Sermon 54

83. How was the Word made flesh and dwelled among us?

In order to speak to others, the thought in our minds changes into a sound, called speech which, through the ears of the listener, enters the latter's mind. In this transition our thought is not changed but remains entire in itself as it passes into speech in order to penetrate the listener's ears. The thought does not deteriorate in the process. In like manner, the Word of God was not changed as it assumed flesh in order that He might be with us.

Christian Doctrine 1, 13

84. How can I praise God always?

An Emperor orders soldiers in his army to do various projects. He commands one soldier to guard the prisoners. He asks another soldier to survey the area for signs of the enemy. He bids another soldier to lead a detachment of the army to destroy a bridge.

As the Emperor uses his army to carry our various tasks, so Christ dwelling in my heart by faith uses my invisible virtues as His army to move my tongue, my hands and my feet to praise God. This invisible army is made up of the virtues of mercy, charity, piety, chastity, and sobriety. Acts of these virtues are always to be performed, whether I am in public or in my home, whether I am talking or keeping silent, whether I am doing an external activity or am free from activity. My external members performing these virtuous acts are seen; Christ within ordering these acts is known only by Christ and myself.

So Christ in my heart by faith employs these virtues as His ministers so that I can praise God always.

Epistle of John to the Parthians 8, 1

85. Should we forgive those who injure us?

Jesus on the Cross asked His Heavenly Father to forgive those who crucified Him because they did not know what they did. Therefore, we should forgive our enemies in order to imitate Christ's forgiveness of His persecutors.

On Psalm 70, 3

86. Why did Christ visit us?

There is a big difference between a prisoner in jail and the friend visiting the culprit. For a time they are both in prison. But, at the end of their conversation the prisoner remains in prison, and the visitor leaves the jail to live as a free person.

Before the Incarnation all human beings were incarcerated due to original sin. When Christ came into the world He visited the cap-

tives. For a time, both Christ and human creatures were together in prison. By shedding His
blood upon the Cross Christ not only left the
prison of this world but also released all human
persons from the imprisonment of original sin.

Although now we live a short, mortal life,
Christ has given us hope for an eternal life in
Heaven.

Epistle of John to the Parthians 2, 10

87. *How may we come to Christ?*

If a person on board a ship anchored perma-
nently in the ocean sees his native land from a
distance, and also notices the intervening water, such an individual has no way of going
ashore. The sea prevents this person from coming to the mainland.

Christ comes to the rescue and provides a
tree by which such a person may traverse the
water. This tree is the Cross of Christ. No one
can cross the sea of life unless carried by the
Cross. Whoever does not depart from Christ's
Cross will arrive at the true native land, Heaven.

On the Gospel of John 2, 2

88. Do all the texts of the Old Testament speak of Christ?

In a harp the musical sounds come from the strings not from the other parts of the harp. When these strings are tuned, the harpist plucking the strings produces beautiful music. The rest of the harp connects the strings.

Similarly, the Old Testament texts either foretell a future event, Christ, or they unite texts that predict His coming.

Against Faustus the Manichee 22, 94

89. How did the Apostles come to know that Christ is God, the King of the Universe?

Tobit's son held his father's hand so that Tobit, lacking bodily sight, might walk safely. Yet blind Tobit had an inner sight by which he taught his son the rules for living a good life. Hence the son's bodily sight was inferior to his father's inner eye.

In a similar way, the Apostles, with their outer eyes, saw Christ eating at the house of Levi, drinking water from the well in Samaria, apprehended, scourged, crowned with thorns, nailed to a cross, wounded by a spear, died and was buried. When the Holy Spirit came to the Apostles, with their inner eye they recognized that Christ was God, the King of the Universe.

Hence the Apostles' outer sight by which

they viewed Christ's bodily life was inferior to
their inner eye illumined by grace by which they
knew that Christ was God, the King of the Universe.

On the Gospel of John 13, 3

90. Why does Christ attract every person?

If you extend a tree branch covered with leaves
a brief distance before a sheep, the sheep will
run toward the foliage. If you hold up a box of
nuts in front of a child, the child will reach for
the delicacies. In like manner, Christ, the Truth,
allures the spiritual appetite of all persons seek-
ing truth, wisdom, righteousness and eternity.

On the Gospel of John 26, 5

91. Why will Christ's followers always walk in the light of Christ?

On an all-day excursion the sun will accompany
you from dawn and will leave you at dusk to
continue your journey in darkness. Even though
Our Lord Jesus Christ is not visibly present to
you, He is whole everywhere; if you do not depart from Christ, He will not depart from you.

On the Gospel of John 34, 6

92. How may we compare Christ with the sun?

The sun is greater than the stars because only the sun provides daylight. Moreover, Christ is greater than all the saints and wise men.

But there is a difference in the comparison. For there is a certain distance between the sun and the stars. But far greater is the distance between Christ and all the saints and wise men.

Letter 14 to Nebridius

93. How can the infant body of Christ emerge without opening His mother's womb and afterwards penetrate closed doors?

There are many examples of tiny creatures having great power. God has given ants and bees better sight than asses and camels. The Creator has enabled the tiny seed of a fig tree to develop into a tree with huge branches; yet larger seeds grow into smaller plants. Consider how God has endowed a human person. The power of sight in the minute pupil of the eye gazes on the whole sky. One spot in the brain provides the activity for all five external senses. The organ of the heart gives life to all the parts of the human body.

Is it any wonder that the power of Christ explains Christ's birth without opening His mother's womb, as well as Christ's passing through closed doors?

Letter 137 to Volusian

94. *How can we love Christ?*

If you are caught in the river of time and are drifting down the rapids, you have a choice. Either you may drown in the water, or you can catch hold of a tree by the stream and save your life. Similarly, you have a choice in the world. Either you may love the world that passes away with time, or you may hold on to Christ and live eternally with God.

Epistle of John to the Parthians 2, 10

95. *How may we learn in the school of Christ?*

Two persons may examine a beautifully hand-written manuscript of a Latin Bible. The first person, ignorant of the Latin language, by the power of sight sees the beauty of the handwriting and praises the book. Since the viewer does not know the Latin language, the viewer's mind cannot comprehend the meaning of the text. A second person, well versed in the Latin language, both sees the beauty of the characters and also understands the meaning of the verses. Such a person praises both the characters and their meaning. Some witnesses of Christ's miracles admired them but did not grasp their meaning. Others both praised the miracles and also understood their significance. Those persons in the latter category can learn in the school of Christ.

Sermon 48, 3

96. *How can Christ comfort us?*

A storm tossed boat carried the Apostles and Christ. That Jesus remained sleeping during the rough weather alarmed the Apostles. They knew that He is the Creator and Ruler of the wind. Therefore, they awakened Him. Christ awoke and ordered the wind to subside; and at once the sea became calm.

If suffering enters your life, and you do not recall Christ's sufferings, Christ is sleeping in your heart. Awaken Christ; remember that Jesus endured many tribulations. Now Christ is helping you. Perhaps you may rejoice because by enduring trials you resemble your suffering Savior, Jesus. Calm has returned to your heart.

On Psalm 55, 9

97. *Why did Christ choose His own betrayer as an Apostle?*

Christ chose Judas as an Apostle to give us an example of patience. Just as Jesus patiently received Judas' betrayal kiss, so we must patiently accept the unintentional harm inflicted on us by other persons.

On Psalm 34, Sermon 1

98. How may Christ free us from resentment?

We may do a favor for a friend. Not only does the supposed friend not express gratitude but may even repay us evil for good. Resentment naturally wells up in our heart.

How may Christ help us dispel this resentment? Christ prayed for His persecutors: "Father, forgive them for they know not what they do." Christ has returned good for evil. Likewise we should pray not for ungrateful persons but for ourselves: "Father, help us have no resentment, conscious or unconscious, towards ungrateful persons but love them with the love of Jesus." Thus with Jesus we have returned good for evil.

On Psalm 109, 5

99. How does Christ counsel us to avoid the malice in the world and attain eternal life?

Before Christ's birth evil advisers urged human beings to swim in the filth of depraved morals and be overwhelmed. Then Christ came into the world and planted His Cross, firm and high, giving counsels that enabled us to avoid moral evil and attain eternal life. Christ advised voluntary poverty, kindness, chastity, concord, justice, true filial love not only that we might avoid leading a depraved life but that we may attain eternal life.

Letter 138 *to Marcellinus*

100. Why must we place all our hope in Christ?

At dawn the sun shines on the mountains. As the day progresses the sun lights up the lowest places on the earth.

When Christ came, he first enlightened the Apostles, the mountains. They, in turn, illumined other persons, the sheltered valleys on the earth.

If you want help, the great preachers, the mountains, will assist you. But they give only what they received from Christ, the Sun.

Therefore, we must put all our hope in Christ alone.

On Psalm 35, 9

· XVII ·

Mass

101. Why should attending Mass involve making an internal act of faith?

A person saying vocal prayers internally thinks about the meaning of the words recited. This same person attending the external Sacrifice of the Mass, at the same time, internally believes the great truth made sacramentally present by the Holy Mass: Christ offers His death on the Cross to the Father for the salvation of everyone.

City of God 10, 19

ST PAULS

This book was produced by St. Pauls/Alba House, the Society of St. Paul, an international religious congregation of priests and brothers dedicated to serving the Church through the communications media.

For information regarding this and associated ministries of the Pauline Family of Congregations, write to the Vocation Director, Society of St. Paul, P.O. Box 189, 9531 Akron-Canfield Road, Canfield, Ohio 44406-0189. Phone (330) 702-0396; or E-mail: spvocationoffice@aol.com or check our internet site, www.albahouse.org